What Kind of Animal is it?

Birds

of all Kinds

Rebecca Sjonger & Bobbie Kalman

🌲 Crabtree Publishing Company

www.crabtreebooks.com

Created by Bobbie Kalman

Dedicated by Robert Wainio
To papa's three girls, Mikaela, Alyssa, and Kaitlyn

Editor-in-Chief
Bobbie Kalman

Writing team
Rebecca Sjonger
Bobbie Kalman

Substantive editor
Kelley MacAulay

Editors
Molly Aloian
Robin Johnson
Reagan Miller
Kathryn Smithyman

Design
Katherine Kantor
Margaret Amy Reiach (cover)
Robert MacGregor (series logo)

Production coordinator
Katherine Kantor

Photo research
Crystal Foxton

Consultant
Patricia Loesche, Ph.D., Animal Behavior Program,
Department of Psychology, University of Washington

Illustrations
Barbara Bedell: pages 4 (cardinal and red grouse), 5 (penguin),
    8 (owl), 10, 14, 16, 18 (eggs), 22, 27, 28 (bottom), 29, 30,
    32 (middle row-far left and right and flying)
Katherine Kantor: pages 6, 7, 31, 32 (vertebrates)
Jeannette McNaughton-Julich: page 4 (top-left and right)
Margaret Amy Reiach: page 32 (nests)
Bonna Rouse: pages 5 (all except penguin), 12, 15, 18 (booby),
    20, 24, 25, 26, 28 (top-left and right), 32 (top row and chicks)
Doug Swinamer: pages 8 (wing), 11, 32 (feathers)

Photographs
Dennis Nigel/Alpha Presse: page 11
Other images by Adobe, Corel, Digital Stock, Digital Vision,
    Eyewire, Image Club Graphics, and Photodisc

Crabtree Publishing Company

www.crabtreebooks.com   1-800-387-7650

Copyright © 2005 CRABTREE PUBLISHING COMPANY.
All rights reserved. No part of this publication may be
reproduced, stored in a retrieval system or be transmitted in
any form or by any means, electronic, mechanical, photocopying,
recording, or otherwise, without the prior written permission
of Crabtree Publishing Company. In Canada: We acknowledge the
financial support of the Government of Canada through the Book
Publishing Industry Development Program (BPIDP) for our
publishing activities.

Cataloging-in-Publication Data
Sjonger, Rebecca.
  Birds of all kinds / Rebecca Sjonger & Bobbie Kalman.
    p. cm. -- (What kind of animal is it?)
  Includes index.
  ISBN-13: 978-0-7787-2160-4 (RLB)
  ISBN-10: 0-7787-2160-4 (RLB)
  ISBN-13: 978-0-7787-2218-2 (pbk.)
  ISBN-10: 0-7787-2218-X (pbk.)
  1. Birds--Juvenile literature. I. Kalman, Bobbie. II. Title. III. Series.
  QL676.2.S58 2005
  598--dc22   2005000498
                                                    LC

**Published in
the United States**
PMB16A
350 Fifth Ave.
Suite 3308
New York, NY
10118

**Published
in Canada**
616 Welland Ave.,
St. Catharines, Ontario
Canada
L2M 5V6

**Published in the
United Kingdom**
73 Lime Walk
Headington
Oxford
OX3 7AD
United Kingdom

**Published
in Australia**
386 Mt. Alexander Rd.,
Ascot Vale (Melbourne)
VIC 3032

Contents

➤ Birds of all kinds ⤸

A bird is an animal that has a beak and feathers. There are many kinds of birds. Birds live all over the world. How many kinds of birds do you know?

cardinal

red-winged
blackbird

Some birds **perch** in trees. To perch means to sit. Cardinals and red-winged blackbirds perch in trees.

red grouse

Some birds stay close to the ground. They almost never fly! Red grouses stay close to the ground.

Some birds hunt and eat other animals. Bald eagles hunt and eat other animals.

bald eagle

emperor penguin

Canada goose

Some birds cannot fly. Penguins and ostriches cannot fly.

ostrich

Some birds live near water. Geese live near water.

Bird bodies

Birds have two wings and two legs. They are **warm-blooded** animals. The bodies of warm-blooded animals stay warm, even in cold places.

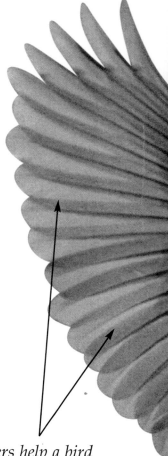

Feathers help a bird fly. Feathers also keep a bird's body warm and dry.

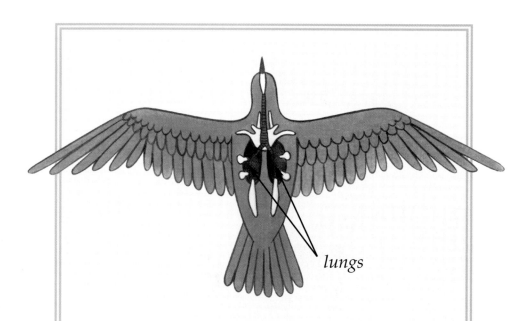

lungs

Breathing air

All birds must breathe air to stay alive. Birds breathe air using **lungs**. Lungs are body parts that take in air. They also let out air. All birds have two lungs.

A bird has two feet. It uses its feet to walk. A bird may also use its feet to carry food.

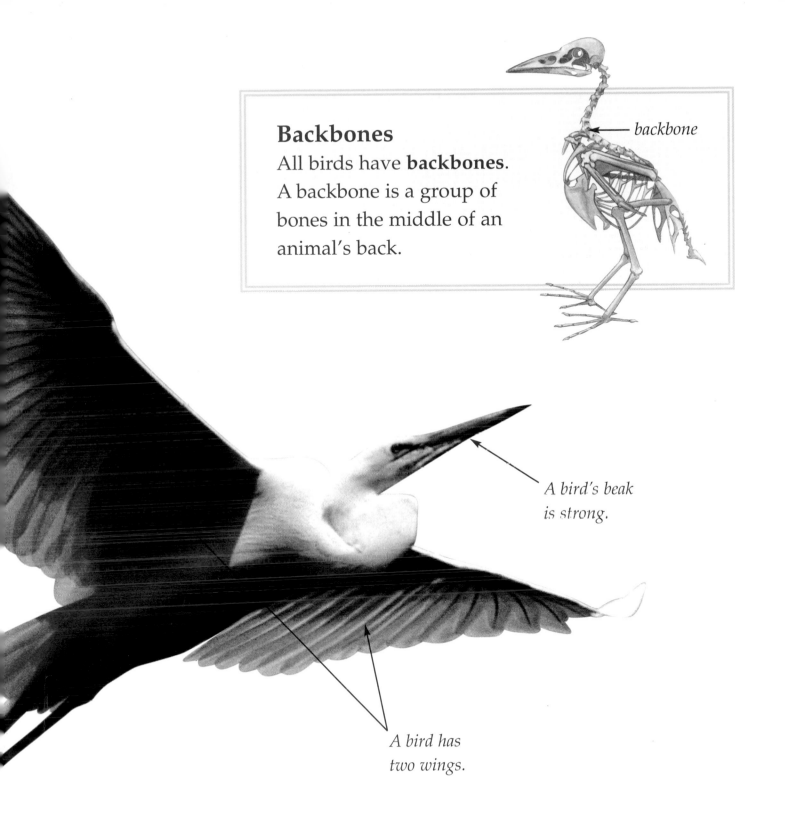

Backbones

All birds have **backbones**. A backbone is a group of bones in the middle of an animal's back.

backbone

A bird's beak is strong.

A bird has two wings.

Feathers

Birds are covered with feathers. They have soft fluffy feathers near their skin. These fluffy feathers are called **down**. Down keeps birds warm.

Flying feathers

Birds also have strong, stiff feathers. These feathers cover the soft feathers. Stiff feathers help birds fly.

This baby hawk is covered in down. When it gets older, its flying feathers will grow on top of its down. The bird will then look like the adult hawk beside it.

Birds that fly have strong, stiff feathers on their wings.

So many colors!

Different birds have feathers of different colors. Some birds have feathers that help the birds hide. The colors of the feathers match the places where the birds live. Other birds have bright, colorful feathers. Male peacocks have colorful feathers. The bird below is a male peacock.

Some owls hide in trees when they hunt or sleep. The colors of their feathers help the owls hide.

Made for flying

Most birds can fly. Birds use their wings to take off and land. In the air, birds **flap** their wings to move and turn. Birds flap their wings by moving them up and down.

Birds must flap their wings many times to take off.

A light body

A bird has **hollow bones**. Hollow bones have empty spaces inside them. Hollow bones make a bird's body light. Having a light body helps a bird fly.

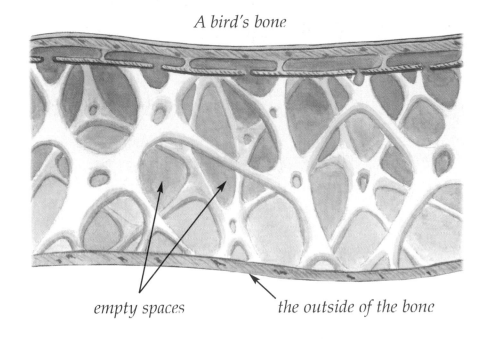

A bird's bone

empty spaces　　　*the outside of the bone*

Why birds fly

Flying helps birds stay alive. When birds cannot find food in one place, they can fly to another place to find food. Birds also fly when other animals are hunting them. The birds on the left are flying away from a jackal that is looking for dinner!

What do birds eat?

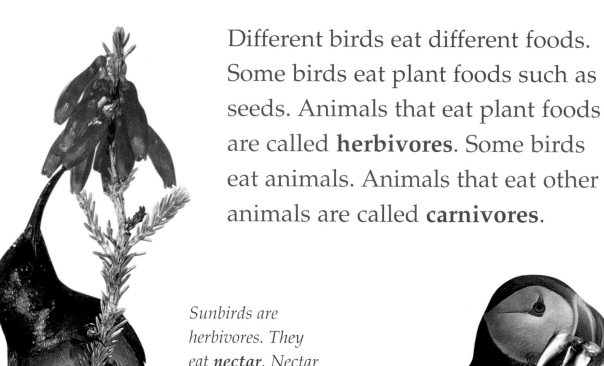

Different birds eat different foods. Some birds eat plant foods such as seeds. Animals that eat plant foods are called **herbivores**. Some birds eat animals. Animals that eat other animals are called **carnivores**.

*Sunbirds are herbivores. They eat **nectar**. Nectar is a sweet liquid found in flowers.*

Puffins are carnivores. They eat fish. How many fish did the puffin find for food?

Finding food

Birds do not like to share their meals with other birds! Most birds look for food alone, but some birds look for food in groups. Looking for food in groups can help birds find more to eat.

The birds in this picture are common terns. Common terns sometimes look for food in groups.

Feeding babies

Some young birds need their parents to feed them. The parents fly away to find food. They bring back the food to their babies. The young birds open their mouths when their parents return with the food. The parents drop small pieces of food into the mouths of the babies.

🐦 Birds all over 🐦

Birds live almost everywhere on Earth. They make homes in dry places, in wet places, in warm places, and in cold places. The natural places where animals live are called **habitats**. Some bird habitats are forests, fields, deserts, and places that are near water. Some birds even live in the coldest parts of the world, such as Antarctica!

Birds that live in warm places often have brightly colored feathers.

Penguins live in the freezing waters of Antarctica.

Time to fly!

Some birds live in places where the winters are cold. When the cold weather comes in autumn, most of these birds fly to warm places. The warm places are far away. The birds stay in the warm places for winter. They fly back home in spring.

Canada geese live near water. They fly to warm places before the water freezes.

@ Nest sweet nest! @

This bird has some grass in its beak for making a nest.

Most birds make **nests**. Nests are warm, safe places where birds lay their eggs. When the babies hatch from the eggs, they live in the nests. Some nests are hidden in leafy trees and plants. Others are hidden on the ground. Birds hide their nests so other animals will not eat their eggs or babies.

This nest is on the ground. The grasses and dirt around the nest help hide it.

Nest builders

Nests can be many shapes and sizes. Different kinds of birds make nests using different things. Birds may use leaves, twigs, feathers, and mud to build their nests.

This weaver used straw to build its nest. The nest looks like a basket.

These egret parents have made a nest from branches and leaves.

Eggs and chicks

robin's egg

tern's egg

pheasant's egg

osprey's egg

Not all bird eggs are the same size or color, but most eggs are oval-shaped. The oval shape makes eggs strong. Eggs must be strong because parent birds sit on the eggs. Sitting on the eggs keeps the **chicks** inside warm. Chicks are baby birds.

cassowary's egg

A booby warms its eggs with its feet.

18

Young birds

After the chicks hatch, they stay in their nests. Some chicks stay in the nests for a few weeks. Others stay for a few months. Parent birds keep their chicks warm and safe in the nests. Most parents stay with their chicks until the young birds are ready to live on their own.

These baby hawks will stay in their nest until they learn to fly.

In the trees

Birds that perch in trees have long toes. Their toes can curl around the tree branches. Birds that perch build their nests in trees. They find food close to where they live.

Many birds that perch have small bodies.

This bird is called a pied wagtail. It eats insects that live in trees.

Many birds that perch in trees are songbirds. Songbirds can sing! Songbirds sing to find other birds. They also sing to keep some birds away. This mockingbird is a songbird.

wild turkey

 # On the ground

chicken

Some birds live on the ground and hardly ever fly. The wings of these birds are weak, but their legs and feet are strong for walking. Turkeys and chickens are birds that live on the ground. They can fly, but they cannot fly far.

22

Life on land

Some birds that live on the ground build nests near the ground. They also look for food close to the ground. Most of these birds eat plants and insects. This bird is a francolin. It eats berries, plants, and insects.

In the water

Some birds live near rivers, ponds, lakes, and oceans. Many birds that live near water are good swimmers. Birds that swim have **webbed feet**. Webbed feet have skin between the toes. Birds use their webbed feet to paddle in the water. Many birds that swim dive down to find fish and other foods.

webbed feet

Trumpeter swans eat only plants. As they swim, they put their heads down into the water to bite off plants to eat.

Close to land

Some birds make their nests along the water's edge. They find their food in shallow water. These birds have long legs so they can walk in water. Their toes spread wide apart to help them stand in sand and mud. Birds that live along the water's edge have long thin beaks.

Birds that live near the water's edge catch tiny worms and shrimps in their beaks.

Birds that hunt

The bodies of some birds are built for hunting animals. Birds that hunt are good fliers. They have sharp, curved claws called **talons**. They use their talons to catch and carry food. Birds that hunt use their sharp beaks to tear food into pieces so they can eat it.

Bald eagles catch fish and other animals to eat. This bald eagle is about to catch a fish.

Hunting

Some birds hunt during the day. Daytime hunters see very well. They can see the animals they are hunting from high in the sky. Other birds hunt at night. Most nighttime hunters have good hearing. Owls can hear small animals that are moving around in the dark.

Secretary birds catch snakes and other animals to eat. They stomp on the animals using their strong legs and big feet.

A few kinds of birds cannot fly. Birds that cannot fly have big bodies with small wings. Their small wings cannot lift their big bodies into the air. Birds that cannot fly must walk or swim. They have strong legs and feet to carry them.

Penguins flap their wings under water to help them swim.

Cassowaries do not need to fly away from danger. They attack their enemies with their sharp claws.

28

Kiwis have wings, but their wings are very small. You can hardly see them!

Rheas have large wings, but they cannot fly. Sometimes they flap their wings as they run. They flap their wings to change direction!

An ostrich has very strong feet. It can run faster than any other bird can.

Create your own birds

Some birds look different than the birds you usually see. Their feathers may be long or spiky. The feathers of other birds may be very colorful. Most colorful birds live in places with hot weather.

black-crowned crane

quetzal

lilac-breasted roller

Choose different parts

You can create your own
bird by putting the bodies
of two or three kinds of
birds together. Flip
through this book and
look at some birds.

How will your bird look?

Will your bird be colorful or plain?
Will the bird have a long or short tail?
Think about what your bird will eat.
What kind of a beak will it need?
Will it have a long, thin beak or
a short, curved beak?
Will it have long or short legs?
Will your bird have a crown
of feathers on its head?

Draw it and color it

When you have decided on how
your bird will look, draw a picture
of it. Color your picture with crayons
or paint. Have your friends make
up birds, too. Display your bird
art in your classroom, the library,
or in the hallway of your school.

Words to know and Index

backbone

backbone
page 7

birds that cannot fly
pages 5, 28-29

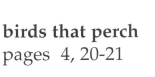
birds that perch
pages 4, 20-21

birds that hunt
pages 5, 9, 26-27

chicks
pages 8, 13, 16, 18-19

webbed feet

birds that live near water
pages 5, 14, 15, 24-25

birds that live on the ground
pages 4, 22-23

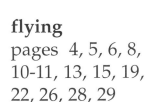

flying
pages 4, 5, 6, 8, 10-11, 13, 15, 19, 22, 26, 28, 29

eggs
pages 16, 18

feathers
pages 4, 6, 8-9, 14, 17, 30, 31

nests
pages 16-17, 19, 20, 23, 25

1 2 3 4 5 6 7 8 9 0   Printed in the U.S.A.   4 3 2 1 0 9 8 7 6 5